Leonardo DiCaprio,
c/o CAA,
9830 Wilshire Boulevard,
Beverly Hills,
CA 90212,
U.S.A.

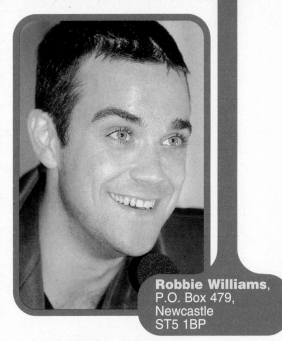

Robbie Williams,
P.O. Box 479,
Newcastle
ST5 1BP

SOAPS

Brookside,
Campus Manor,
Childwell Abbey Road,
Childwell,
Liverpool L16 OJP

EastEnders,
c/o BBC Elstree Centre,
Clarendon Road,
Borehamwood,
Herts WD6 1JF

Grange Hill,
c/o Room N117,
BBC Elstree Centre,
Clarendon Road,
Borehamwood,
Herts WD6 1JF

Home & Away,
P.O. Box 406,
Beaconsfield,
Buckinghamshire
HP9 2HQ

Heartbreak High,
3 Alveston Place,
Leamington Spa
CV32 4SN

Neighbours,
P.O. Box 136,
Watford
WD2 4ND

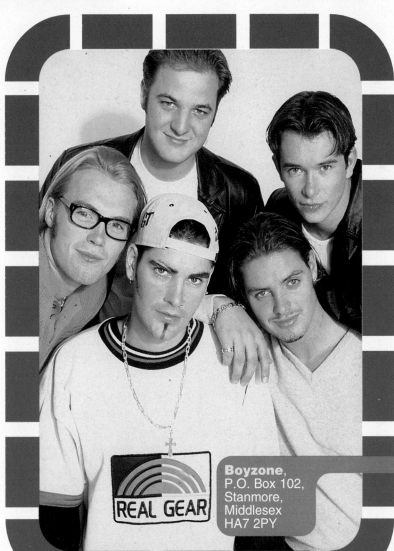

REAL GEAR

Boyzone,
P.O. Box 102,
Stanmore,
Middlesex
HA7 2PY

What's in?

4

We've got it wrapped on page 104.

Jennifer and Sarah put on the glitz on page 93.

"Hi, I'm Laura, and I'm on page 96."

Who cheated? Jacki starts her investigations on page 107.

Stained glass goodies to make. The recipe's on page 113.

Printed and Published in Great Britain by D. C. Thomson & Co., Ltd., 185 Fleet Street, London EC4A 2HS.
© D. C. Thomson & Co., Ltd., 1999   **ISBN 0 85116 700 4**

TEDDY FOR SALE

HI, I'm Zoe. Me and my best mate, Wendy, go into town on Saturday afternoons. We usually look round the shops, like last Saturday —

LOOK, WENDY, ISN'T THAT TEDDY SWEET?

YEAH! HE'S DEAD CUTE!

I'M GONNA BUY ONE — I'VE GOT ENOUGH MONEY.

SO HAVE I — I'LL GET ONE, TOO!

But, in the shop —

I'M AFRAID WE'VE ONLY GOT THIS ONE LEFT.

6

9

11

THE COMP

ONE Christmas term at Redvale Comprehensive, headmistress "Grim Gertie" Grimstyle had good news for the pupils.

THIS CHRISTMAS HOLIDAY THERE WILL BE A CHRISTMAS CRUISE AROUND THE MEDITERRANEAN. IF YOU ARE INTERESTED IN GOING, ASK YOUR FORM TEACHER FOR DETAILS.

ONE Christmas term at Redvale Comprehensive, headmistress "Grim Gertie" Grimstyle had good news for the pupils.

A CRUISE! FANTASTIC!

IT WOULD BE JUST SO COOL TO GO!

WE *HAVE* TO GO, LAURA!

WE'LL HAVE SOME OF THAT, EH, FREDDY MATE?

Basher Bartlett was 9B's form teacher —

MR COLE AND MISS SMITH WILL BE THE TEACHERS ACCOMPANYING THE CRUISE.

SOOTY COLE'S OKAY, CLAIRE.

YEAH, BUT MAD MAUREEN SMITH'S *NOT!* OH, WELL — WE CAN'T HAVE EVERYTHING, NIKKI!

THE CRUISE DEPARTS ON DECEMBER 20TH AND RETURNS DECEMBER 29TH . . .

OH! WE'LL BE AWAY ON CHRISTMAS DAY! I HADN'T REALISED THAT, BECKY!

WE CAN'T GO, HAYLEY. WE'D MISS CHRISTMAS WITH BEN AND TOM, AND LITTLE BLAIR AND HANNAH.

BUT WE CAN SEE OUR LITTLE BROTHERS AND OUR NEPHEW AND NIECE ANY TIME. THIS IS A ONCE IN A LIFETIME CHANCE, SIS!

After school —

I BET THEY'LL SAY WE CAN'T AFFORD IT — NOT WITH TWO OF US TO PAY FOR.

I'M STILL GOING TO ASK! WE'VE JUST GOT TO GO, BECKY!

But —

I'M SORRY, GIRLS. THERE JUST ISN'T THE MONEY. CHRISTMAS IS EXPENSIVE ENOUGH, WITHOUT THIS.

I KNEW IT.

Meanwhile, at Laura's —

THE ONLY THING IS, IT'S OVER CHRISTMAS. WOULD YOU MIND, MUM?

IT'LL BE A WONDERFUL CHANCE FOR YOU, LAURA. AND WE CAN HAVE A SPECIAL NEW YEAR INSTEAD, WHEN YOU GET BACK.

15

EVERYONE ON BOARD, QUICKLY! DON'T DAWDLE!

The next few weeks passed quickly, and almost before the Comp pupils knew it —

HUH! WE'RE ON HOLIDAY AND MAD MAUREEN'S ACTING LIKE A SERGEANT-MAJOR!

MEDITERRANEAN, HERE WE COME!

DO YOU THINK SOMEBODY SHOULD PHONE AHEAD AND WARN THEM ABOUT HODGE AND FREDDY?

But soon, Hayley was feeling unwell.

HAYLEY, YOU *CAN'T* BE SEASICK! WE HAVEN'T EVEN LEFT PORT!

SHE GETS SEASICK IN THE BATH, MR COLE!

OOOGH!

In their cabin —

I BAGS THE TOP BUNK!

OHHHH! I'M STAYING HERE!

THINK SHE'LL BE OKAY?

SHE'LL BE FINE. LET'S CHECK OUT THE SHIP. THE BROCHURE SAID IT HAS A SWIMMING POOL AND A GYM!

WOW! BADMINTON COURTS!

SHAME THERE ISN'T ONE FREE. I'D LIKE A GAME.

HI! I'M NITA AND THIS IS JADE. ARE YOU WITH ONE OF THE SCHOOL PARTIES, TOO?

YEAH, REDVALE COMP.

WE'RE FROM ST AIDAN'S HIGH. FANCY A GAME? WE'LL CHALLENGE YOU!

THEY'RE GOOD — THEY'RE CLOBBERING US!

YOU'LL HAVE TO GIVE US A CHANCE TO GET OUR OWN BACK!

TABLE-TENNIS?

YOU'RE ON!

Soon —

21-17! OUR GAME!

IT'S OUR TURN TO GET OUR OWN BACK NOW! SEE YOU AFTER LUNCH.

WHAT'S WRONG? Find out on Page 87.

SQUARE

PICK A SQUARE AND

Ready Steady Look!

Does READY, STEADY or COOK appear most in our hot happenin' grid?

R	R	Y	D	A	E	T	S
R	E	D	A	Y	C	S	T
Y	A	A	K	O	O	C	E
D	D	E	D	O	O	C	A
A	Y	R	O	Y	K	K	D
E	K	S	T	E	A	D	Y
T	C	O	O	K	O	O	C
S	O	S	Y	D	A	E	R

Cool!

Cross out the letters which appear twice in each square and you'll discover two members of the Simpsons. Which three family members don't appear?

```
V B E M
L S I A
R M V S
E I T L
```

```
O B E L
R M I R
E S O T
A T M B
```

A-Maze-ing!

Which path will lead Chris Evans to the TV in the centre of this maze? A, B, C or D?

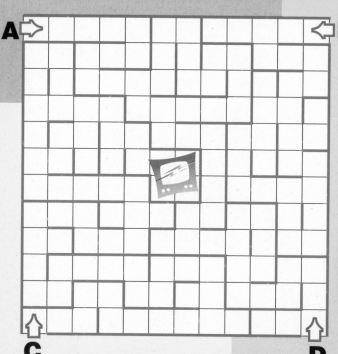

A

B

C

D

20

EYES!

TRY SOME TV puzzles

Family Fun!

Unravel these family names and match them up with their TV soaps!

TAYREBBST

HIKROLLC

EMLCHILT

GINLED

EMMERDALE

EASTENDERS

BROOKSIDE

CORONATION STREET

TV Challenge!

Find the following shows, past and present, in our terrific TV wordsquare: ART ATTACK, BROOKSIDE, BLUE PETER, BYKER GROVE, CASUALTY, EASTENDERS, EMMERDALE, FRESH PRINCE OF BEL AIR, FRIENDS, GLADIATORS, GOOSEBUMPS, GRANGE HILL, HOLIDAY, HOLLYOAKS, KIPPER, LIVE AND KICKING, NEIGHBOURS, NEWSROUND, PARTY OF FIVE, PET RESCUE, ROSEANNE, RUGRATS, SISTER SISTER, SM TV LIVE, SESAME STREET, THE BIG BREAKFAST, THE BILL, THE MAG, THE O ZONE, THE PEPSI CHART, THE SIMPSONS, TFI FRIDAY, TITCH, TOP OF THE POPS, USA HIGH, WIZADORA, ZZZAP.

```
A R O D A Z I W T L L I H E G N A R G F
S K A O Y L L O H A E F R A G E E H S R
T U T E E R T S E M A S E S U I L K I E
A G S B D L L I B E H T P T L G A M S S
R C A A S D N E I R F O P E N H D W T H
G I P M H Q R S G T B U I N V B R X E P
J Y A C E I E F B I R J K D K O E L R R
R B Z D G H G H R G O O S E B U M P S I
S T O P O F T H E P O P S R N R M M I N
R M A R T A T T A C K T U S V S E W S C
O P T O Y Q R S K X S E N O Z O E H T E
T E N V T A B Z F Y I R O S E A N N E O
A U E C L I V E A N D K I C K I N G R F
C W Y A I D F S H E R E T E P E U L B
O S S A U E V G T I B Y K E R G R O V E
A E R D S T H E P E P S I C H A R T N L
L R O I A I J A Y A D I R F I F T M O A
G T U L C T C F Z J L E S U O H N U F I
B E N O E C H Z P A R T Y O F F I V E R
O P D H G H Z I K S N O S P M I S E H T
```

THE FOUR MARYS

THE FOUR MARYS, Cotter, Field, Radleigh and Simpson, friends at St Elmo's School for Girls, were writing out their Christmas cards —

I LOVE CHRISTMAS!

ME, TOO! AND THERE'S THE DISCO NEXT WEEK.

YEAH — WITH THE BOYS FROM ST BARTOPH'S.

St Bartoph's was a nearby boys' boarding school.

ARE *YOU* LOOKING FORWARD TO THE DISCO, MONICA?

NOT MUCH. I DON'T REALLY LIKE DISCOS.

I ALWAYS FEEL LEFT OUT. NO-ONE ASKS ME TO DANCE AND —

I THINK THERE MAY BE A REASON FOR THAT — DON'T YOU, VERONICA?

YES, PROBABLY *SEVERAL*, MABEL.

Snobs, Mabel and Veronica, were the least popular girls in the school.

THERE'S THE HORRIBLE HAIR AND THE SPOTS AND —

SHUT UP, YOU TWO!

MONICA, JUST IGNORE THEM!

IT'S A PITY MONICA'S SO SHY BECAUSE SHE'S REALLY NICE — UNLIKE *SOME* PEOPLE AT THIS SCHOOL!

I KNOW! MABEL AND VERONICA ARE DEAD MEAN!

YOU KNOW, I'M SURE WE COULD MAKE MONICA LOOK REALLY GOOD FOR THE DISCO BUT SHE MIGHT BE OFFENDED IF WE OFFERED.

WELL, LET'S FIND OUT. SHE SHOULD REALISE WE'RE JUST TRYING TO HELP.

And —

THAT'D BE GREAT, THANKS. MY PARENTS ARE AWAY A LOT, SO I'M AT MY GRAN'S WHEN I'M NOT HERE. AND GRAN DOESN'T KNOW MUCH ABOUT MAKE-UP OR FASHION.

WELL, YOU WON'T RECOGNISE YOURSELF WHEN WE'VE FINISHED THE MONICA MAKEOVER!

HEAR THAT?

YEAH! HA! HA!

Next day —

OH, WHY CAN'T THOSE TWO JUST LEAVE MONICA ALONE?

SO HAVE YOU BOOKED SOME SESSIONS AT THE BEAUTY SALON IN TOWN?

NO, SHE HASN'T. SHE DOESN'T NEED ANYTHING LIKE THAT.

ARE YOU *SURE*?

IT'S NOT GOING TO BE MUCH OF A MAKEOVER, THEN!

AND YOU'RE *EXPERTS*, ARE YOU?

OF COURSE! WE KNOW *EXACTLY* WHAT TO DO — AND TO PROVE IT, WE'LL GIVE *OURSELVES* A NEW LOOK FOR THE DISCO!

A few days later —

LOOK! WE'VE JUST BEEN TO GET OUR NEW DRESSES FOR THE DISCO!

ST ELMO'S SCHOOL FOR GIRLS

QUALITY FASHIONS

OH.

DID YOU SEE THEIR BAGS? THEY'VE BEEN TO THAT REALLY POSH SHOP IN ELMBURY! ARE YOU SURE MINE WILL BE OKAY?

YEAH! LIKE MY AUNT, THE DUCHESS SAYS, 'MONEY DOESN'T MEAN STYLE'.

A couple of days later —

MABEL AND VERONICA ARE BUYING HALF THE STORE!

COSMETICS MAKE-UP

HAVE I *REALLY* GOT ENOUGH?

YES, YOU HAVE. STOP WORRYING!

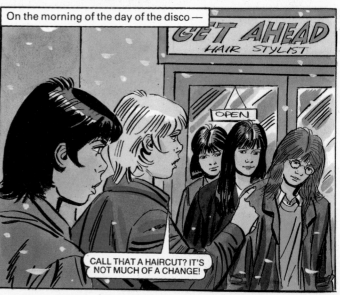

On the morning of the day of the disco —

GET AHEAD HAIR STYLIST

OPEN

CALL THAT A HAIRCUT? IT'S NOT MUCH OF A CHANGE!

25

SAFARI

Flying

The girls are about to see a Boeing 757 undergo a "C" check – a massive overhaul. Maria's aunt, Colette, works for Britannia Airways and she ensures the girls are signed in at Reception.

Colette welcomes the girls aboard a plane with a difference!

Hey! What's happened to all the seats? They've been taken away for cleaning. The carpet's due to come up, too.

Colette shows the girls the galley where the in-flight meals are prepared.

VISIT!

Bunty readers, Samantha Maddox and Maria Hoare, paid a flying visit to Britannia Airways at London Luton Airport.

On the flight deck, Clive, one of the engineers, checks all the instruments.

The girls find themselves a couple of seats!

At the check-in desk ready to welcome passengers aboard.

Departures

LONDON LUTON AIRPORT

Time to go. Now, what did we do with our passports?

Samantha and Maria really enjoyed their visit. Our thanks to Colette and the staff at Britannia Airways for letting us take a peek behind the scenes.

Cat 'N' Mouse Cakes

These cool cakes are easy to make and loadsa fun.

YOU'LL NEED

1 pkt sponge cake mix
1 egg
1 pack of ready to roll icing
Jam
Glacé cherries
Jelly diamonds
Cola lances
Strawberry shoelaces
Choc chips or raisins
Chocolate buttons

WHAT TO DO

1. Follow the instructions on the cake mix pack and bake into small buns (you should get about 12 from the mix). Let your buns cool.
2. Roll out the icing till it's about ½cm thick and use a 5-6cm round cookie cutter to cut circles from the icing.
3. Spread the tops of your cakes with a little jam and stick an icing disc on the top of each one.
4. Now your cakes are ready to decorate. Dab a tiny amount of water onto the icing to help the decorations stick.

CAT

Ears: ½ jelly diamond
Eyes: choc chips or raisins
Nose: ½ jelly diamond or ¼ glacé cherry
Whiskers: strawberry shoelaces (snip them into smaller bits with scissors)

MOUSE

Ears: chocolate buttons
Eyes: choc chips or raisins
Nose: ½ glacé cherry
Whiskers: cola lances (snip them into smaller pieces)
Tail: Strawberry shoelaces

Attach these at the bottom of the cakes by making a small hole through the bun case and into the cake (a cocktail stick is ideal). Add a dab of jam to the end of the shoelace and poke it into the hole.

● *Remember — always ask an adult before using any kitchen equipment.*

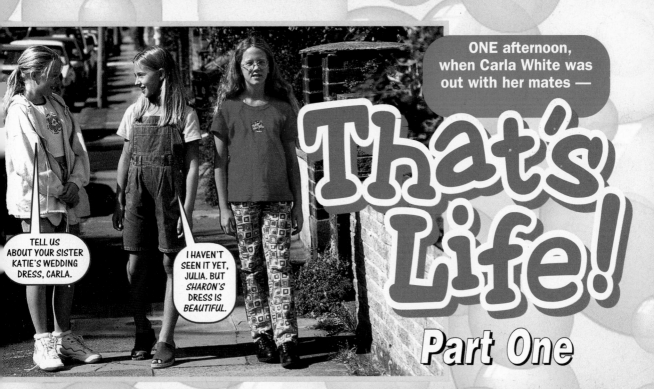

ONE afternoon, when Carla White was out with her mates —

That's Life!

Part One

TELL US ABOUT YOUR SISTER KATIE'S WEDDING DRESS, CARLA.

I HAVEN'T SEEN IT YET, JULIA. BUT SHARON'S DRESS IS BEAUTIFUL.

SHARON? WHO'S SHARON?

YOU KNOW, LEANNE — IN 'FOLK AT HOME'.

WHAT? NOT THAT NAFF SOAP OUR LOCAL TV COMPANY MAKES?

DON'T SAY YOU WATCH *THAT*, TOO — AS WELL AS NEIGHBOURS, CORRIE, EASTIES, EMMERDALE, BROOKIE . . .

I'VE JUST THOUGHT OF A GOOD NICKNAME FOR YOU.

BUBBLES! AS IN *SOAP* BUBBLES!

HA! HA!

IT'S PERFECT — ALL YOU DO IS WATCH SOAPS!

I DO NOT!

YOU DO, TOO! YOU'RE MORE INTERESTED IN THE WEDDING OF THIS SHARON THAN YOUR OWN SISTER'S!

31

33

But, a few minutes later —

It was Katie!

34

35

MORE DRAMA ON PAGE 79!

GIRLS TALKING

CREEPER CREATURES

IT was Gemma Carson's birthday. Because it fell on a school day, she wasn't celebrating with her friends until the weekend.

SO ARE YOU DOING ANYTHING SPECIAL THIS EVENING, GEMMA?

YEAH, MUM AND DAD ARE TAKING ME FOR A PIZZA.

I'D BETTER GO. I'VE TO MEET MUM AT HER OFFICE.

HAVE A NICE TIME!

Shortly —

SORRY, LOVE, I'VE GOT ONE IMPORTANT PHONE CALL TO MAKE. IT WON'T TAKE LONG.

GRAB A CHAIR, GEMMA.

THANKS.

I DON'T SUPPOSE YOU CAN TYPE, CAN YOU?

NOT FAST, NO! I'LL JUST WATCH . . . WHAT'S THAT SCREEN?

JUST THE MONITOR FOR A SECURITY CAMERA WE'VE GOT IN THE CAR PARK. A LOT OF THE CARS WERE BEING DAMAGED.

YEAH, MY MUM MENTIONED THAT.

NOT BADLY — JUST SCRATCHED, MOSTLY! DUNNO WHY — THEY WEREN'T BROKEN INTO OR ANYTHING.

AARGH!

L-LOOK!

DON'T WORRY — IT'S JUST A BRANCH — OR TENDRIL, I THINK THEY'RE PROPERLY CALLED.

OH!

THERE'S A VINE OUT THERE — A CREEPER-TYPE PLANT — AND THE WIND SOMETIMES BLOWS IT IN FRONT OF THE CAMERA.

SORRY, I CAN SEE THAT'S WHAT IT IS NOW. WHAT AN IDIOT! FOR A MOMENT I THOUGHT IT WAS A SPOOKY ARM OR SOMETHING . . .

YOU'RE NOT AN IDIOT AT ALL — IT FRIGHTENED A FEW OF US HERE TOO WHEN WE FIRST SAW IT.

RIGHT, I'M READY! COME ON GEMMA!

40

YEAH, THERE IT IS — THE VINE, BLOWING IN FRONT OF THE CAMERA, JUST LIKE BARRY SAID.

Gemma told her mum what had happened.

I WONDER WHAT IT'D SAY IF IT KNEW WHAT A FRIGHT IT GAVE ME?

PLANTS CAN'T SAY ANYTHING, SWEETHEART! GOSH, I'M HUNGRY. HOPE YOUR DAD'S READY.

At the end of their meal —

BET YOU'RE NOT HUNGRY ANY MORE!

YOU'RE RIGHT! I THINK I'VE HAD TOO MUCH!

But that night, as Gemma slept —

AARGH!

GOSH, WHAT AN AWFUL DREAM! I MUST HAVE HAD TOO MUCH PIZZA!

A year later, Gemma's birthday was again in the middle of the week.

HAPPY BIRTHDAY, LOVE!

I KNOW YOU'RE HAVING YOUR FRIENDS ROUND ON SATURDAY, BUT LET'S GO FOR A PIZZA TONIGHT, SAME AS LAST YEAR, JUST TO CELEBRATE ON THE DAY ITSELF.

41

MEET ME AT WORK AGAIN, LIKE LAST TIME.

GREAT! THANKS!

So, after school —

I WON'T BE LONG. JUST ONE PHONE CALL TO MAKE.

JUST LIKE LAST YEAR, ISN'T IT?

NOT *QUITE* THE SAME . . .

. . . AT LEAST *THIS* YEAR I KNOW THAT'S JUST THE VINE!

DON'T EAT TOO MUCH!

DON'T WORRY, I'M NOT GOING TO!

LAST YEAR I HAD A REALLY BAD . . . HANG ON —

— THE VINE'S BEEN CUT RIGHT BACK! IT'S NOW OUT OF RANGE OF THE CAMERA!

SO W-WHAT WAS IT I SAW ON THE SCREEN?

COME ON, OR WE'LL BE LATE FOR YOUR DAD.

ER . . . YEAH . . . OKAY, MUM.

I MUST HAVE JUST IMAGINED IT . . . I MUST HAVE!

Luckily, Gemma did not turn round.

GONE THEY HAVE.

GOOD . . . HARD IT IS WHEN THEY COMINGS AND GOINGS. BUT ALWAYS HERE TONIGHT WE CELEBRATES.

SINCE LONG BEFORE *THEM* CAME HERE . . .

GEMMA WILL ENJOY HER BIRTHDAY MEAL. I HOPE SHE DOESN'T EAT TOO MUCH AND GIVE HERSELF NIGHTMARES!

THE END

SUSIE flopped back on the sofa as the video ended.

"Aw!" she sighed. "It was the boy next door she fancied all the time. That's dead romantic! No chance of that happening to me — there *isn't* a boy next door!"

"What about the boys who live in your street — all that lot who get on the school bus?" asked her mate, Emma. "Some of them are quite tasty!"

"You're joking!" cried Susie, sitting up. "Name *one!* And I don't live in a street — it's Canterbury *Close,* remember!"

"Okay, okay! Anyway, there's that blond guy from Year Ten. There's Carl from our year, but he's always clowning about. And Stuart Barton from the French Circle. And what about that shy boy who always sits at the back with a crowd of mates? Hey — and there's . . ."

"Hang on!" Susie said, laughing. "That's enough to be going on with!"

"I don't know what you're complaining about," smiled Emma. "*I* wouldn't mind having all those boys living in *my* street — sorry, close!"

Susie thought hard as she walked home. Maybe she *should* take a better look at the local talent. If it wasn't to be the boy next door, why *not* the boy from the close?

Next day, the usual group of boys were at the bus stop. Stuart was with them. He wasn't really that bad-looking. If you half shut your eyes, you could almost say he looked a bit like Leonardo DiCaprio. She smiled at him as they got on

the bus for school.

"Hi, Stuart! Going to the French Circle at lunchtime?"

"Er — well — yeah," he said, turning red.

"Me, too. See you then," said Susie. She sat down, feeling pleased with herself. Wait till Emma heard about this! After all, it didn't do any harm to *make* things happen, did it?

"So, how did it go?" Emma asked Susie after lunch.

"Brilliant!" said Susie. "He asked me to be his partner in one of the games and then he asked me for a date! We're going bowling on Saturday!"

"Cool!" grinned Emma. "Looks like you've made a hit

already! What did I tell you? All those cute guys living in your close and you were ignoring them! Give me a ring on Sunday — I'll be dying to hear how it went."

*   *   *   *

"No, no, *no!*" Susie wailed into the phone on Sunday. "It was awful! Stuart Barton's a *mega*-bore!"

Emma made sympathetic noises. "What happened then?"

"He just went on and on about how marvellous he is at French and how all the French girls fancied him on holiday. *And* he's the world's worst at bowling, too!"

"Looks like you'll have to try again," said Emma. "Who's next?"

"Carl, I think."

Susie knew Carl was keen on table-tennis, so on Saturday morning, she and Emma turned up at the sports centre. Sure enough, Carl was there with his mate, waiting for a table.

"Hi, Carl!" said Susie, smiling innocently. "Fancy meeting you here! You play a lot?"

"Yeah!" replied Carl. "We're pretty good, aren't we, Lee?"

"Huh! I bet we could beat you!" said Susie. "Losers buy the Cokes, okay?"

"You're on!" grinned Carl.

Later, as Susie paid for the drinks in the café, Carl said, "You're not too bad for a girl, you know. Why don't you join the table-tennis club?"

"I might just do that," said Susie. "Brilliant!" she thought. "Carl *must* be interested!"

A moment later, there was a scream and Emma jumped up from her chair. A huge black spider had appeared on the floor beside her.

Susie and Emma clung together, with horror. But then they realised Carl and Lee were doubled up, laughing.

"Caught you!" giggled Carl. "You girls are dead soft — you fall for that trick spider every time!"

"Stupid clown!" said Emma on the way home. "How juvenile, trying to scare us with a plastic spider!"

"Yeah," Susie agreed. "That Carl's a total waste of space!"

*   *   *   *

After that, Susie had almost decided to give up on any idea of dating a 'Boy from the Close', when something happened to change her mind. At a birthday party for one of her cousins, Susie bumped into Damon, one of those very boys.

"Hi, Susie!" he said. "Fancy a dance?"

"Er — yes!" said Susie, astonished that he knew her name, never mind that he was asking her to dance! Damon had never even spoken to her before!

Susie noticed how different Damon looked. He was really cool, in black jeans and a leather jacket — *much* better than his school uniform.

It was the best party Susie had ever been to. She and Damon stayed together for the rest of the evening! He even walked her home in the moonlight — just like in the films. But he didn't ask her out. He just said he'd see her on the bus on Monday morning.

On Monday Damon waited for Susie when they got off the bus. United were playing a big game that evening, he said, and he had two tickets — would she like to go with him? Susie hated football, but with Damon smiling at her like that, how could she refuse!

So, on Monday they went to the match, on Tuesday the skating rink, on Thursday the cinema and on Saturday she dumped him.

"*What?*" said Emma in amazement. "But why? I thought he was *the one!*"

"So did I," sighed Susie. "It'd have been okay if it'd just been him and me, but wherever we went *all* his mates showed up, too — it was like dating a football team!"

*   *   *   *

Next day Susie walked along the close. She thought of all the other boys who lived there. Adam was a year younger than her, Robin always had a packet of crisps in his hand, and Paul was a right nerd.

"I'll give the rest a miss," she told Emma as they watched a slushy video that evening. "Maybe I'll meet the right guy on holiday. That'd be *much* more romantic than dating the boy next door!"

The End.

TIME BUSTERS!

Nothing to do? No money? Completely bored? Well, fret no more, our 10 great ideas will keep you busy, busy, busy!

1 Have a big clear-out. It may sound dull, but once you start to uncover things you'd forgotten you had it'll be a laugh. Did you really wear those pink and lime striped leggings?

2 *Ask your mates to do the same and when you've finished you can swap some of the things you don't want. Give anything that nobody wants to charity. That way you've helped out AND earned Brownie points for having a tidy room.*

3 Get a bit of rope or old washing line and skip yourself fit. Skipping's an excellent way to exercise. It's fast, fun and FREE!

4 *Need to give someone a pressie and you're totally skint? Get some pieces of pretty paper and write a promise on each one. The promises could be anything from buying your mate a choccy bar to giving your mum some peace and quiet or walking the dog in the rain for your dad. Pop the promise vouchers into a card and that's it.*

5 Paint each toenail a different colour of nail polish for smiley, happy feet.

6 *It may sound obvious, but try a new hobby. Libraries and community centres often have lists of what's on in your area. Check them out and soon you could be doing anything from Saturday morning art classes to trampolining.*

7 Want a brand new look? Go to a training night at a hairdresser's. Don't worry, you won't be clipped bald by someone who's never lifted scissors before. All trainees are well supervised by qualified stylists. You could end up with a brill new style for less than a fiver!

8 *Make memory boxes to store all your precious bits 'n' pieces. Cover an old shoe box with some cool wrapping paper (or give it a lick of paint) and have fun filling it up. You can put in all sorts of things – photos of you and your mate, cinema tickets from a first date, sand in a jar from your summer hols or anything else you like.*

9 Go to a car boot sale with some pals. There are lots of sales now, so you're sure to find one near you (look for notices in your local paper). It's amazing what you can pick up for as little as 50p. Go early for the best bargains.

10 *Make lots of funky things from salt dough. It's easy and they're great for pressies. All you need to do is mix one cup of salt with two cups of plain four. Add enough water (a little at a time) to make a soft, but not sticky, dough.*
Now use the dough to make little models. Stick one piece to another with a dab of water. Or roll it out and cut into shapes for earrings, brooches, fridge magnets and hanging on the wall. Air-dry your dough in a warm place for 2-4 days or slow-bake in a cool oven (140ºC, 275ºF, Gas Mark 1) for 2-3 hours. When the dough is dry, you can paint and varnish it.

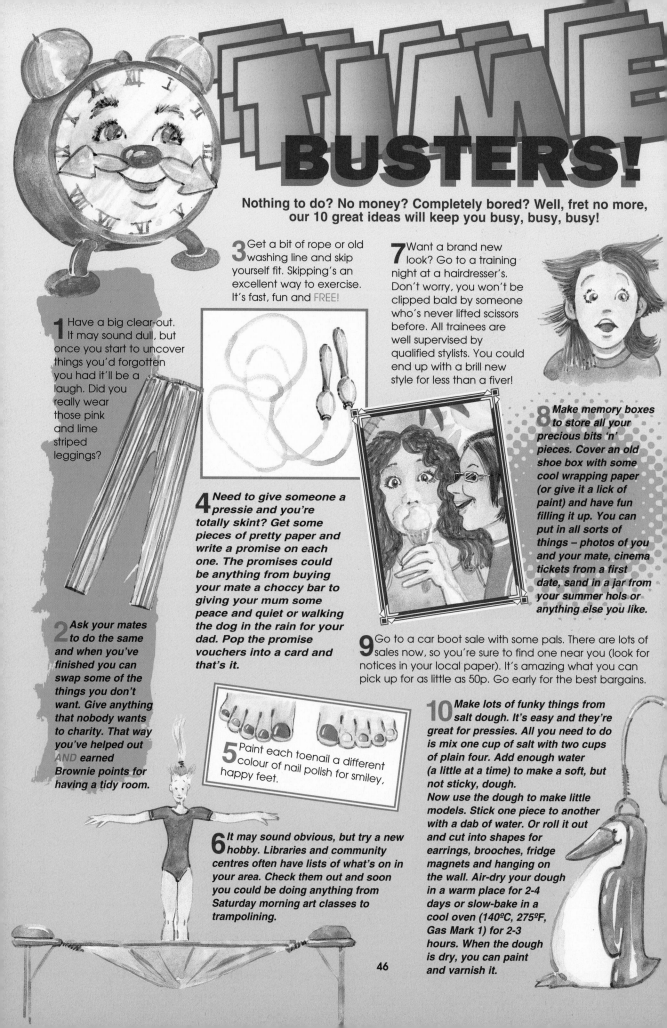

47

48

EXCUSE ME, YOU WERE LOOKING AT THE SCI-FI BOOKS IN THE SHOP WHEN I WAS IN, WEREN'T YOU?

ER...

I THINK HE'S TWIGGED I'M FOLLOWING HIM! OH, LOIS, THIS IS A RIGHT MESS YOU'VE GOT ME INTO!

IT'S JUST I'M A BIG SCI-FI FAN, TOO, AND I WONDER IF YOU'D READ ANYTHING PARTICULARLY GOOD RECENTLY?

ER — NO, NOT RECENTLY.

NOT EVER. I HATE ALIENS AND ALL THAT!

Ben chatted to Carina while they waited.

AH, HERE'S MY BUS.

THE HOSPITAL BUS. DO YOU LIVE NEAR THERE?

NO. BUT MY COUSIN'S IN HOSPITAL WITH A BROKEN LEG AND I VISIT HIM MOST AFTERNOONS. HE GETS BORED. SEE YOU.

YEAH. SEE YOU.

HE'S NICE. IT'S HARD TO BELIEVE HE'S CHEATING ON LOIS.

49

Later — ...AND HE DIDN'T MEET ANY GIRL, LOIS. I THINK YOU'RE WRONG.

WELL, LET'S SEE WHAT HAPPENS TOMORROW. YOU SAID YOU'D DO IT FOR A FEW DAYS.

Next day —

HE'S THERE WAITING FOR THE HOSPITAL BUS AGAIN. I'D BETTER GET ON IT TOO THIS TIME, SO I CAN CONVINCE LOIS THAT REALLY IS WHERE HE'S GOING. ONE OF MY AUNTS LIVES OUT THAT WAY. I'LL CALL AND SEE HER.

Once again Ben and Carina got talking and, when they arrived at their destination —

THE JOURNEY'S JUST SPED PAST TODAY WITH YOU TO TALK TO. I CAN'T BELIEVE WE'RE HERE ALREADY!

IT HAS GONE QUICKLY.

At Carina's aunt's —

IT'S LUCKY YOU POPPED IN TODAY. I'VE GOT ON TWICE AS FAST WITH MY DECORATING WITH YOU HERE TO PLAY WITH SAMMY.

I'LL COME BACK TOMORROW, IF YOU LIKE.

Next day —

HERE WE ARE AGAIN!

YEAH.

50

HOW LONG DO YOU STAY AT THE HOSPITAL?

I USUALLY GET THE 4 O'CLOCK BUS BACK.

Later —

TIME YOU WERE OFF, CARINA. DIDN'T YOU SAY YOU WANTED TO CATCH THE 4 O'CLOCK BUS?

OH, YEAH!

And suddenly Carina realised something —

THE REASON I WANT TO GET THE 4 O'CLOCK BUS IS BECAUSE I WANT TO SEE BEN! THIS IS RIDICULOUS! I'M SUPPOSED TO BE KEEPING AN EYE ON HIM FOR LOIS AND I'VE GONE AND FALLEN FOR HIM MYSELF!

When they got back into town —

ARE YOU GOING TO YOUR AUNT'S TOMORROW?

I DON'T KNOW.

IT'S BEST I DON'T. I'LL HAVE TO TELL LOIS TO GET SOMEONE ELSE TO SPY ON BEN. I WON'T TELL HER WHY, OF COURSE!

SHAME. I WAS GOING TO ASK YOU TOMORROW IF YOU WANTED TO COME OUT WITH ME AT THE WEEKEND. I'M GOING OUT WITH SOMEONE AT PRESENT, BUT I'VE MADE UP MY MIND TO FINISH WITH HER TONIGHT. WE'RE NOT RIGHT FOR EACH OTHER.

52

SAFARI

53

DO NOT DISTURB!

▼ READER Elaine Eldridge lets us take a peek inside her room.

● Elaine reads a letter from her pen friend, Tabitha, all the way from South Africa!

● Certificates for disco and jazz dance competitions line her bedroom wall.

● Time for a spot of karaoke. Elaine has her own machine.

● As well as dancing, Elaine loves cheer-leading and she has won numerous trophies and medals.

● A workout with the pom-poms. Elaine cheers for her local club, Luton Town.

● Elaine often challenges her older brother, Graeme, to a game of chess. Your move, Elaine.

● Elaine shows us her brilliant collection of baseball caps.

● Finally, Elaine changes outfits for a spot of disco practice. Thanks for letting us into your room, Elaine.

55

ROOM 13

IT was spring half-term and Carly Walker and her parents were taking a short holiday in Dorminster—

IT'S A LOVELY OLD TOWN, ISN'T IT? NOW, TURN LEFT — THE WOODVIEW HOTEL'S ALONG THERE.

WOODVIEW — IT SOUNDS LOVELY.

But—

HM, IT LOOKED A LOT BETTER IN THE BROCHURE, MUM.

YES, IT'S NOT VERY INVITING. NEVER MIND, WE'RE HERE NOW AND WE'LL ENJOY SEEING THIS PART OF THE COUNTRY.

WELCOME TO WOODVIEW. I'M MRS GREAVE. I HOPE YOU'LL ENJOY YOUR STAY IN MY HOTEL. CHECK IN, THEN I'LL SHOW YOU TO YOUR ROOMS.

THERE'S SOMETHING A BIT CREEPY ABOUT HER, LIKE HER HOTEL.

57

59

FAY'S FUTURE

ONE afternoon, when Fay Marshall was in the park with her mates —

AAAAAH!

FAY!

I — I MUST HAVE COME THROUGH ANOTHER EXIT FROM THE PARK! BUT — BUT I DIDN'T THINK THERE *WAS* ANOTHER EXIT. IT — IT LOOKS EXACTLY LIKE THE ONE I USUALLY USE.

Fay began to feel scared —

WHAT'S GOING ON? OOH! IF ONLY MY HEAD WASN'T SO SORE. I CAN HARDLY THINK.

HI, FAY. I'M JUST FINISHING THAT BOOK YOU WANT TO BORROW.

HI.

WHICH BOOK? AND WHO IS *HE*? I DON'T RECOGNISE HIM AT ALL.

HE SEEMS TO KNOW *ME*, THOUGH.

AND IN NORMAL CIRCUMSTANCES I'D BE PLEASED TO KNOW HIM, TOO. HE'S *CUTE!*

BUT THIS *ISN'T* NORMAL! HAS HITTING MY HEAD AFFECTED MY MEMORY OR SOMETHING?

Fay closed her eyes and tried to think more clearly.

LET'S START AT THE BEGINNING. I WAS IN THE PARK AND . . .

WHAT? THIS IS WHERE I *SHOULD* BE — ON THE OPEN LAND! BUT THE SHOPPING PRECINCT'S GONE!

THE END

Veterinary Surgery
Consultations by Appointment only.

24 Hour Emergency Service
Telephone (01582) 723521

Additional car parking at rear.
Approach via Malzeard Road.

Hollie meets up with her mum in the consulting room and Summer seems to take an instant liking to Mandy, the vet.

Mandy just has to look at a screen to find out all her patients' medical history.

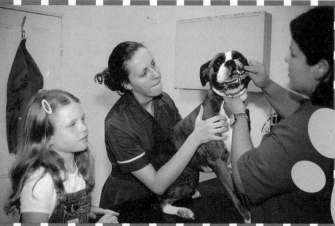

Summer only needs her teeth scaled. Summer's not keen, so Auntie Vicky's called in to help!

Hollie thinks this might be a good time to get out! So she leaves them to it and has a chat with Lyn at the reception desk.

R'S DAY

HOLLIE HIBBERT'S pet boxer, Summer, needed a check-up, so Hollie took her along to the local vet's, where her Auntie Vicky is a veterinary nurse.

Afterwards, Auntie Vicky shows Hollie around the surgery. In the lab, Hollie looks at some blood samples — oo-er!

Then on to the X-ray room. X-rays can show a lot of things – especially if the animals have eaten something they shouldn't have!

Next door is the operating theatre. Hollie's auntie shows her the anaesthetics trolley. It's like something out of Casualty!

With a clean bill of health, Hollie and her pet say goodbye and Summer thanks Auntie Vicky with a big sloppy kiss!

Many thanks to Mr Owen Pinney and the staff at the surgery.

Fancy That!

MICHELLE FOSTER'S family had moved house and it was her first day at her new school.

HELEN WILL LOOK AFTER YOU, MICHELLE, AND HELP YOU SETTLE IN.

OKAY, THANKS!

Later, at break —

YOU OKAY, MICHELLE?

THAT'S MY BROTHER, SCOTT. HE'S JUST STARTED IN YEAR NINE.

A few days later —

YOUR BROTHER'S REALLY NICE, MICHELLE. DO YOU THINK I STAND A CHANCE WITH HIM?

YOU AND SCOTT? I DON'T KNOW, HELEN, BUT I'LL SEE WHAT I CAN DO.

OH, THERE HE IS! GO AND TALK TO HIM NOW, MICHELLE.

I CAN'T, HELEN. I'VE GOT TO GET THIS HISTORY FILE BACK TO RACHEL, BUT I'LL TALK TO HIM TONIGHT.

69

70

Soon —

COME ON! LET'S GO AND GET A DRINK.

NO, THANKS. I'M GOING TO KEEP LOOKING FOR SCOTT. I'M BOUND TO SEE HIM SOON AND THEN YOU CAN GET US TOGETHER.

Then, in the café —

SCOTT! WHAT ARE YOU DOING HERE?

DON'T LOOK SO SURPRISED! I THOUGHT I'D GIVE IT A TRY WITH MY MATES.

WE THOUGHT OF GOING TEN-PIN BOWLING, BUT THEN WE DECIDED TO COME HERE INSTEAD.

ENJOY YOURSELVES THEN.

I'D BETTER GET BACK TO HELEN — AND QUICK!

HELEN, I'VE JUST SEEN ONE OF SCOTT'S FRIENDS AND I THINK SCOTT AND THE OTHERS ARE GOING BOWLING.

WHAT? BUT I'VE NO MONEY LEFT! WE CAN'T GO!

DON'T WORRY, I'LL PAY. NOW HURRY.

71

BACKSTREET BOYS WIN. THEY'RE GREAT!

I WANT TO LOOK AT SOME JEWELLERY NEXT. EARRINGS, I THINK.

OOOH! THAT DOG'S JUST LIKE BUSTER. BRILLIANT.

Hours later —

HI, BUNTY. IS THAT YOUR SHOPPING FINISHED?

WELL, SORT OF, LISA.

I'VE BOUGHT ALL THE THINGS *I* WANT, SO I'LL START ON PRESENTS FOR OTHER PEOPLE *TOMORROW!*

HA, HA, HA!

75

POP QUIZ!

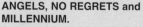

IN THE BOX

Solve the clues to find some pop peeps and then see if you can fit their names correctly into the grid. We've given you two letters to start you off.

1. You might find these gorgeous guys hanging out in Florida.
2. He's had singles called ANGELS, NO REGRETS and MILLENNIUM.
3. Wayne, Mark, Dane and Bobak are on this.
4. He sings, he's cute, he's blond and he's Nick BACKSTREET's bruv.
5. A name for Victoria, Mel C, Mel G and Emma.
6. These goody goody girlies know where it's at.
7. WORDS was this band's first No. 1 hit.
8. Will this pop laydee give you some HONEY TO THE B?
9. Mmm, three lovely brothers make up this band.
10. There's an H in this band — but not in their name.
11. Keavy B*WITCHED's twin sis.
12. We've GOT THE FEELING that this band's brilliant.
13. Brian BACKSTREET's other name.
14. Splash out with this mad Danish band.

CROSS EYED

Cross out the letters that appear three times to find a queen of pop.

Q	M	S	C	A
P	K	D	E	K
O	C	P	E	Q
E	S	K	N	P
Q	N	C	A	S

Cross out the letters that appear three times to find a pop lay-dee who's married to one of BOYZONE. Who is she married to and which group is she in?

W	E	D	C	W
Y	C	Y	K	A
D	K	S	C	O
T	W	O	H	Y
K	E	O	D	R

WHO AM I?

Can you guess who these pop stars are from the descriptions?

1. I have long brown hair and I like casual clothes. I have had two albums and lots of hit singles. I am signed to Madonna's record label, Maverick. I am very miserable, THANK YOU very much.
2. I am the youngest in a band of three brothers. I have blond hair. I play drums. I am very loud and shout a lot.
3. I am over 50 and have long hair. Sometimes I wear wigs. I first had hits as part of a duo in the sixties. ... have had lots of hit singles and acted in a lot of films, too. One of my films was called MERMAIDS. I like to wear some really strange outfits.
4. There are three of us in the band We've had lots of hits like MORE THAN A WOMAN and FRIDAY NIGHT. We come from Carlisle. Our names are Lee, Spike and Jimmy.
5. I come from a very famous family. My brother is one of the most successful pop stars of all time. He has a ranch called NEVERLAND. My three nephews also have a band. I love dancing and I've had lots of hits.

TRUE OR FALSE?

Some of these facts are true and others are completely made up. Do you know which are which?

1. Lisa STEPS celebrates her birthday on Bonfire night.
2. Posh Spice was once chucked out of WH Smith when fans following her caused a big rumpus.
3. Keith BOYZONE and his wife opened a new cosmetic store in Dublin last year.
4. Mel C sang a duet with grannies' fave Daniel O'Donnell.
5. Lindsay B*WITCHED collects socks and has to buy a pair in every country the girlies visit.
6. CHER's real name is Cherylin Sarkasian La Pier.
7. LeAnn Rimes' granny is the famous country singer, Dolly Parton.
8. Scott FIVE was a champion ice skater when he was young.
9. Radio One's Zoe Ball has a famous dad who used to present maths and science progs on TV.
10. Chris Evans and Will McDonald are planning to release a record called GINGER WHINGER.

DISC-O

Solve the musical clues and fill in the CD. The last letter of each answer is the first letter of the next one. We've given you the first letters to start you off.

1. You might go to a music studio to make one of these.
2. An instrument with strings.
3. Where you might hear a song being played.
4. All the pop peeps would like their record to reach this number.
5. How you might feel if yours did.
6. CD is short for COMPACT - - - -.
7. You can hear these on the radio every Sunday.

SPOT THE STARS

Help! Something's gone wrong! Can you tell who these popstrels are?

IN THE MIX

Unscramble these letters to reveal some stars, then match them up with one of their songs.

1. FUPF ADDDY	ALL THAT MATTERS
2. LATAINE AILGUBIMR	COMMON PEOPLE
3. OLISUE	WONDER WALL
4. LPPU	TORN
5. ASIOS	I'LL BE MISSING YOU

Part Two
Continued from Page 35.

That's Life!

It was Grandad —

79

But, that night —

By morning, there was still no news.

Carla told her mates all that had happened.

THE END

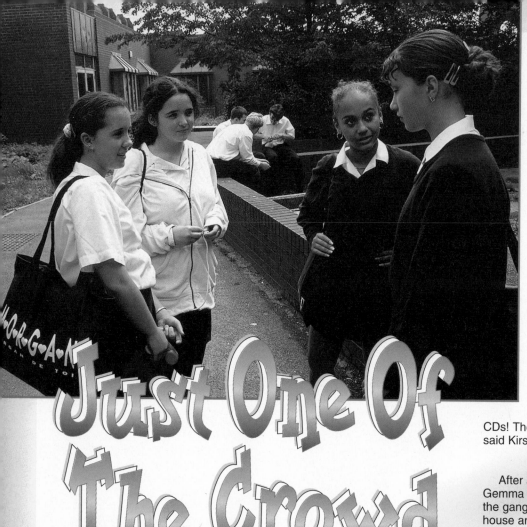

Just One Of The Crowd

WHO'S the new girl?" Kirsty whispered to her two friends as they filed into the assembly hall. A slim girl with fair hair was being shown along the corridor.

"I don't know, but she looks dead nervous!" Stephanie noted. "It can't be much fun starting at a new school in the middle of term."

"Kirsty!" Their teacher stopped them. "This is Gemma. She's new today so I'd like you to look after her. Will you take her into Assembly?"

"Yes, of course," said Kirsty. She grinned at Gemma. "Come on, Gemma — we'll show you round!"

All day Kirsty and her friends guided Gemma round the school and filled her in with snippets of school gossip. Gemma relaxed, and when the bell rang at four o'clock she was laughing with the girls as if she'd been at the school for years.

"Where do you live?" asked Kirsty. "The gang's coming round to my house tonight. Do you want to come and join us?"

Gemma hesitated.

"We live on the other side of town . . . but I'd *love* to come, Kirsty. I'll get a lift."

"Great!" Kirsty grinned at her. "See you then — and bring your fave CDs!"

* * * *

That evening the girls watched out for Gemma.

"Here she is now," said Anne. "Oh, she's *walking*. That's odd — didn't she say she'd get a lift?'

"My gran brought me," Gemma explained later. "But she dropped me at the corner of the street."

"I'm glad you made it," Kirsty said. "Have you brought any CDs?"

Gemma opened her bag and tipped a pile on to Kirsty's bed.

"I just grabbed a few," she said. "What do you want to hear?"

"Wow!" said Anne. "Are all those yours?"

"Yeah," said Gemma. "Play any of them you want."

The time passed quickly and it didn't seem long before Gemma glanced at her watch.

"Oh, no! It's eight already!"

"Can't you stay any longer?" asked Kirsty. "No-one's come for you yet."

"I'm meeting Gran at the corner," Gemma explained, gathering up her CDs. "That's what we arranged because we weren't sure where you lived. Thanks for asking me!"

"See you tomorrow!" called Kirsty, as Gemma hurried off.

When she had turned the corner, Stephanie spoke with the others.

"Did you see Gemma's trainers? They must have been dead expensive."

"Yeah! And all those CDs! They'll have cost a packet," said Kirsty. "Lucky Gemma!"

* * * *

After a few days it seemed like Gemma had always been one of the gang. They met at Stephanie's house and then at Anne's and then at the weekend, they decided

84

to go for a bike ride.

"Tell us where you live, Gemma," said Kirsty. "We can cycle round and collect you."

"Oh, no!" said Gemma quickly. "I'll come over here to meet you."

"It's a long way," Kirsty said, looking doubtful.

"I know, but I'd rather do that," said Gemma firmly.

Later, when Gemma had gone, Stephanie spoke up.

"It's odd that Gemma's never said where she lives. It's almost like she doesn't want us to know."

"Yeah," Kirsty agreed. "*I'd* wondered too, but I expect she'll invite us round soon. She's visited all of us, so it's her turn now."

* * * *

On Saturday morning Gemma arrived early at the meeting-place.

"Wow!" said Anne. "That's a dead classy bike you've got, Gemma!"

"You're lucky," said Stephanie enviously. "My old crock belonged to my brother. I'd *love* to have a really nice bike."

"Me, too," sighed Anne. "Mine was my cousin's old one. Don't you get things passed down, Gemma?"

Gemma shook her head, smiling.

It was a good day out. The weather was perfect and the girls cycled to a country park where they ate their picnic. Gemma in particular seemed to enjoy herself, screaming and laughing the loudest when the girls splashed one another in the stream. And when they passed the refreshment kiosk she insisted on treating the others to huge ice creams with as many toppings as they wanted.

Later, when they were back at Kirsty's house, Gemma smiled.

"That was a really great day! You're the best friends I've ever had!"

As she rode away, the others looked at one another.

"Did you hear that?" said Kirsty. "You'd think she'd never had any friends before."

"It's weird that Gemma never talks about her family," Stephanie added. "We don't even know if she's got any brothers or sisters."

"We don't know *anything* about her," agreed Anne. "She said once her parents were often away on business and her gran looks after her, but we don't know where she lives. She hasn't invited us round to her house yet."

"I'm sure she will soon," said Kirsty. "Then we'll find out all about her."

* * * *

But the days passed and there was still no invitation from Gemma. She was always ready to treat her friends when they were out together, and she joined in eagerly with all their plans, but she *never* talked about her family or home.

"It's boring talking about me," she would say, and before the others realised, they were talking about something else.

One day, on the way to school, Anne confided in the others.

"Gemma told someone yesterday she has a pony. She's never said anything about a pony to us, has she?"

The other two looked astonished.

"A pony? Wow! But why hasn't she told *us?*" asked Kirsty. "We're supposed to be her friends."

"She shouldn't have any secrets from us if she's in our gang," Anne exclaimed. "Hey, why don't we do some detective work and find out where she lives?"

"Yeah!" said Kirsty. "That'd be a bit of a laugh. And Gemma wouldn't have to know."

* * * *

Next morning Kirsty was taking the class register to the secretary's office when an idea struck her. Gemma's address would be in the register! She quickly took a look, and there it was — Farhaven Lodge, Chesterton Avenue.

When she told them, Anne and Stephanie were impressed.

"*That* was easy," said Anne. Then there was a pause. "Er — why don't we cycle round there? Er — just to have a look, of course," she added hastily.

"Yeah, we could," agreed Stephanie. "But only to have a look."

So, that evening, the three girls cycled slowly along Chesterton Avenue.

"That's Farhaven Lodge there!" Kirsty pointed to a huge house set back from the road. "Wow! It's absolutely *enormous!* And there's a swimming pool at the side!"

While they stood looking at the house, an expensive car turned into the drive. It stopped at the front door and Gemma came running out. As she greeted the man and woman who stepped out of the car, Anne gave a squeak of excitement.

"That's Paul and Maria Sheraton! They're on the TV 'Wake Up' show!"

"They must be Gemma's mum and dad! Wow! No wonder she lives in such a big posh house!" said Kirsty. "But why has she kept quiet about it? She could have *told* us."

"Just wait till we tell her we know who she is!" Stephanie said. "That'll be a big surprise!"

Next day the three girls were waiting for Gemma.

"Your mum and dad are on TV, aren't they?"

"Why didn't you tell us you were famous?"

"That's dead exciting!"

Then they stopped when they saw Gemma's face.

"How did you find out?" Gemma demanded, almost in tears. "I didn't want anyone to know. It was great just being an ordinary girl here and having fun like everyone else. I wanted to be just one of the crowd. Now you've spoiled *everything!* "

"Oh! I'm — I'm sorry," said Kirsty. "We didn't mean to upset you."

But Gemma had turned and walked away.

Next morning the class teacher announced that Gemma wouldn't be back because her family was moving away. Kirsty and the other two exchanged glances.

"That's *our* fault. I feel really bad about it," Kirsty whispered to her friends. "Why did we try to be so clever? She just wanted to be like us, but we ruined it for her. Poor Gemma! She thought we were her friends!"

THE END

The first port of call was Gibraltar —

DON'T STAND TOO CLOSE TO THE APES, GIRLS. THEY BITE.

YEAH, DON'T STAND TOO CLOSE. WE CAN'T TELL YOU APART!

VERY FUNNY, DAVID HODGSON!

LOOK AT THIS, CLAIRE! A CLOCK IN THE SHAPE OF THE ROCK! TACKY OR WHAT?

I KNOW! LET'S HAVE A CONTEST — SEE WHO CAN FIND THE NAFFEST SOUVENIR!

HOW ABOUT THIS? GROSS!

NO, THIS!

ROCK & ROLL

Back on the ship —

THERE'S THE WINNERS! HODGE AND FREDDY AND THOSE YUKKY SHADES!

DON'T TELL US YOU ACTUALLY BOUGHT THOSE!

HEY, THESE ARE DEAD COOL!

OUCH!

HA! HA! THEY'RE SO CHEAP YOU CAN'T EVEN SEE THROUGH THEM, HODGE!

Later —

THERE'S THE ST AIDAN'S LOT. WE'VE *GOT* TO PAY THEM BACK FOR ALL THEIR TRICKS!

SSH! MAD MAUREEN'S BEHIND US! SHE'LL HEAR YOU!

YOU KNOW, GIRLS, WHEN I WENT ON A SCHOOL CRUISE ONCE WE TIED THE OTHER SCHOOL'S DOOR HANDLES TOGETHER.

B-BUT OUR CABINS DON'T HAVE DOOR HANDLES, MISS SMITH.

THE CHANGING ROOM DOORS AT THE SWIMMING POOL DO! OF COURSE, I WOULDN'T WANT TO GIVE ANYONE IDEAS . . .

AND JADE AND NITA WERE GOING SWIMMING!

Soon —

THEY'RE COMING OUT OF THE POOL, LAURA.

RIGHT, BECKY, NOW WE WAIT TILL THEY GO TO THE CHANGING ROOMS.

Then —

2

HANDY THAT THEY HAD SKIPPING ROPES IN THE GYM, WASN'T IT?

GOOD OLD MAD MAUREEN. I'LL NEVER CALL HER STUFFY AGAIN!

1

2

HEY! MY DOOR'S STUCK!

SO'S MINE! *LET US OUT!*

ONLY IF YOU CALL OFF THE PRACTICAL JOKES!

89

The girls agreed.

QUITS?

QUITS!

Spain was the next port of call —

I'VE BEEN HERE ON HOLIDAY BEFORE. THERE'S THIS BRILLIANT SHOPPING MALL NOT FAR FROM HERE!

LEAD THE WAY, CLAIRE!

Soon —

THE CLOTHES HERE ARE FAB!

BET YOU'RE GLAD YOU CAME WITH US, JADE!

Later —

WE'D BETTER BE GETTING BACK. WE ONLY HAVE THREE HOURS ON SHORE.

OKAY, IT'S THIS WAY.

OR IS IT . . . THIS WAY?

CLAIRE! DON'T TELL US YOU DON'T KNOW THE WAY BACK!

WHERE IS THE HARBOUR, PLEASE?

OH, GREAT! NO-ONE SPEAKS ENGLISH!

WE'RE LOST! THE BOAT WILL GO WITHOUT US!

But, just then —

GIRLS! OVER HERE!

SOOTY COLE! OH, THANK GOODNESS.

COME ON, GIRLS, THE BOAT WILL SAIL WITHOUT YOU.

SORRY, SIR. IT WAS ALL MY FAULT.

Back on board —

IT'S CHRISTMAS DAY TOMORROW. BEN AND TOM AND THE BABY TWINS WILL BE HANGING UP THEIR STOCKINGS NOW!

WE ALWAYS TURN ON THE TREE LIGHTS ON CHRISTMAS EVE.

MY BROTHER, MAX, ALWAYS RATTLES ALL THE PRESENTS TO TRY AND GUESS WHAT THEY ARE.

AND MY LITTLE BROTHER PUTS OUT MINCE PIES FOR SANTA AND CARROTS FOR HIS REINDEER.

WE-WE WON'T SEE THE LITTLE ONES OPENING THEIR PRESENTS. CHRISTMAS JUST WON'T BE CHRISTMAS WITHOUT OUR FAMILIES!

YOU WERE THE ONE WHO WANTED TO COME! SHUT UP OR YOU'LL START US BLUBBERING!

I JUST WISH I COULD SEE MUM . . .

CHEER UP, EVERYONE! THE CAPTAIN'S GOT A SURPRISE FOR YOU ALL IN THE RADIO ROOM!

Young faces look great without make-up, but Christmas is a good time to go a bit wild.

Shine On!

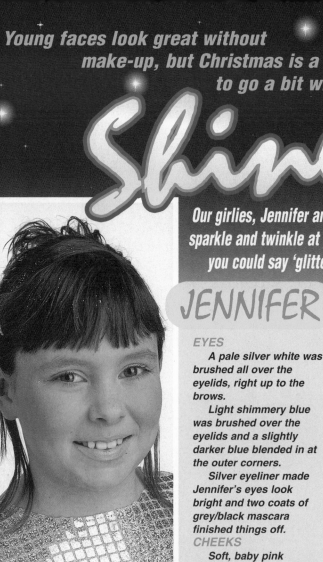

Our girlies, Jennifer and Sarah, wanted to sparkle and twinkle at parties, so before you could say 'glitter' we showed them how!

FACES & BASES

There's no need to trowel on foundation. All fresh faces need are a natural tinted moisturiser. This will even out your skin tones and hide any red bits without looking like a mask. It'll also make your skin lovely and soft. A very light dusting of powder will help your make-up stay put.

JENNIFER

EYES

A pale silver white was brushed all over the eyelids, right up to the brows.

Light shimmery blue was brushed over the eyelids and a slightly darker blue blended in at the outer corners.

Silver eyeliner made Jennifer's eyes look bright and two coats of grey/black mascara finished things off.

CHEEKS

Soft, baby pink blusher gave Jennifer a healthy glow.

* To get your blusher in the right place, blow your cheeks out (like you're blowing up a balloon) and put a little blusher on the fattest bit.

LIPS

A pale, frosty pink was matched to one of the colours in Jennifer's sparkly dress.

HAIR

It's easy-peasy to do this style. Pull your hair back into a low pony-tail (leave some bits out at the sides) and then start to twist it. Keep twisting until you've twisted it all, then twist it up the back of your head. Secure the twist with hair pins or kirby grips. Spike up the ends with a little hairspray.

FINISHING TOUCHES

Glitter everywhere! Glitter gel was smoothed on Jennifer's hair and glitter clips to match her dress added at one side.

More glitter gel was added at the top of her cheeks for lots of Christmas sparkle.

(BEFORE)

(BEFORE)

SARAH

EYES

Pale lilac was brushed all over Sarah's eyelids, up to the brows.

Silvery blue was added to the inner corners of the lids.

A deeper, shimmery blue/purple was brushed on at the outer corners. Two coats of blue/black mascara gave Sarah party eyes.

CHEEKS

Sheer, rosy blush gel was rubbed on to Sarah's cheeks. (Apply gel to the same part of your cheeks as before.)

LIPS

Shiny, candy pink lip gloss finished off the make-up.

HAIR

Sarah has lovely thick, bobbed hair, so we just used a hot brush to flick out the ends.

FINISHING TOUCHES

More glitter — and sequins! Two tiny star-shaped sequins were stuck to Sarah's cheeks at the corners of her eyes (use a tiny blob of hair gel to do this).

Blue glitter was sprayed to the front of her hair and a sparkly star clip added to match her make-up.

GET THE LOOK

You'll be spoiled for choice with all the groovy glitter make-up that's in the shops.

Glitter gel for hair, cheeks and shoulders comes in all sorts of colours and you only need to use a tiny bit for lots of shine.

Add shimmer powder to eyes and cheeks or mix it with a little clear lip gloss for super shiny lips.

Chunky, pearly eye pencils are great. Smooth on eyelids and blend in with your finger or a cotton bud, then use it as an eye-liner, too. They don't take up much space in your bag.

Glitter nail polishes are go! Available in tons of colours for sparkly fingers. There are lots of shiny two-tone colours, too. Try white/gold, blue/purple or grey/silver.

Have instant party hair with bright streaks of hair mascara or spray-on hair paint. You can go wild and wash it out easily before bed.

Get funky!

GET DRESSED!

Even if you don't like dressing up too much, there are brill casual styles with a party look. From shiny combats and silver trousers to metallic coats, there's loads to choose from.

If you love a party look, go for it! Come Christmas the shops are burstin' at the seams with sequins, shimmer and shine. Add a sparkly tiara to finish things off.

DO NOT DISTURB!

HI! I'm Laura Smith and my hobbies include playing the guitar, singing, collecting china dolls and disco dancing. Come inside!

I've been playing guitar for three years now but I still need to practise.

These valuable Steiff bears live in my room, but they belong to my mum.

Some of the trophies I've won for disco and jazz dancing.

This is how it's done!

I've been collecting china dolls for some time. Here are a "few" of them.

I like reading, too, and I get lots of peace and quiet in my room.

97

Sandie's Dad had bought a garage.

BEN'S GARAGE
QUALITY VEHICLE REPAIRS

THANKS, SANDIE. THAT'S THE RIGHT SPANNER FIRST TIME! YOU'RE GETTING GOOD AT THIS!

IT'S ALL READY FOR YOU.

THANKS. I'M LOST WITHOUT MY CAR.

I'M GLAD I'M ABLE TO HELP DAD, BUT I STILL FEEL A BIT JEALOUS WHEN I THINK OF MY MATES HAVING A GOOD TIME.

THERE'S GEMMA AND RACHEL COMING BACK FROM THE BEACH NOW.

HIYA, SANDIE.

DID YOU KNOW IMIJE HAVE STARTED THEIR TOUR?

'COURSE I DID! THEY'RE MY FAVE BAND.

SO ARE YOU COMING TO SEE THEM?

100

IT *IS* IMIJE! WH-WHAT ON EARTH ARE *YOU* GUYS DOING HERE?

WE WERE ON OUR WAY TO OUR CONCERT WHEN THE CAR STARTED MAKING A FUNNY NOISE.

DON'T WORRY. MY DAD'LL FIX IT. HE'S A BRILLIANT MECHANIC.

AND SHE'S A BRILLIANT ASSISTANT — WHICH IS WHY SHE'S NOT AT YOUR CONCERT. SHE STAYED TO HELP ME WITH A BIG JOB. BUT DON'T WORRY, I'LL DO YOUR CAR FIRST.

And soon —

THERE! THAT'S FINE NOW.

I WONDER . . . COULD I HAVE YOUR AUTOGRAPHS?

HANG ON. WE CAN DO BETTER THAN THAT!

SMILE!

I CAN'T BELIEVE THIS — *ME* BEING PHOTOGRAPHED WITH *IMIJE!*

GOT YOU!

AND EMMA THOUGHT SHE WAS DOING ME A FAVOUR BY SAYING SHE'D BLOW MARK A KISS FOR ME! I CAN'T WAIT TO TELL THEM ABOUT *THIS!*

WE'LL SEND THE PHOTOGRAPHS SOON.

Next day —

OH, SANDIE, IT WAS BRILLIANT!

I'LL NEVER FORGET IT!

ACTUALLY, I HAD QUITE A NIGHT MYSELF!

102

Sandie told them what had happened.

. . . AND MARK GAVE ME A *KISS!* I HAVEN'T WASHED MY FACE SINCE!

OH, YEAH?

IS THAT RIGHT?

THEY DON'T BELIEVE ME! I WAS SO LOOKING FORWARD TO TALKING ABOUT IT, BUT THEY THINK I'M MAKING IT UP.

Later —

YOU'RE QUIET, SANDIE. STILL THINKING ABOUT YESTERDAY?

YEAH.

AND ABOUT RACHEL AND EMMA THINKING I WAS MAKING IT UP.

Then, next day —

GOOD, WE'VE GOT THE BUTLER'S CONTRACT! OH, AND THERE'S A LETTER FOR YOU, TOO.

IT'S FROM IMIJE! THEY'VE SENT ME THE PHOTOS LIKE THEY PROMISED *AND* TICKETS FOR THEIR NEXT SHOW!

I WONDER WHAT THE GIRLS' FACES WILL BE LIKE WHEN THEY SEE THIS! THEY'LL *HAVE* TO BELIEVE ME NOW!

THE END

Well Wrapped!

You've done all your Crimbo shopping, now fo[r] the wrapping. So how d'you make even the cheapest pressie look like a million? Easy — just follow our instructions.

FAIRY GOOD

Make some easy-peasy fairies to decorate your parcels and you can hang them on the tree afterwards.

You'll need glittery or coloured pipe cleaners, large beads or cotton craft balls (around 5p each), sequin waste (around 20p a metre) and a tiny piece of feather trim (or left-overs from your feather duster). All these things are available from fabric shops or art and craft shops.

Starting at one end, fold the sequin waste strip into a fan. Do around 15 folds, each about 1.5cm wide. Cut off the left-over sequin waste. Pinch the fan at the bottom and push a pipe cleaner through the holes. Twist it to secure the ends. Make another fan (about 10 folds) and pinch it together in the middle. Push the pipe cleaner through to attach the skirt to the wings. Push the bead or cotton ball on for the head and fold back the left over pipe cleaner to make a hanging hook. Draw on a face and glue feathers for hair.

FLUFFY

Feathery things are big news, but scalping your big sis's feather boa is NOT what to do. We bought a cheap feather duster (99p from a discount store) and unwound the tape that held the feathers on. Now just wrap your pressies in plain paper and decorate with feathers held on with double-sided sticky tape. Simple!

RECYCLE

Go green and make great wrapping out of old corrugated cardboard packaging, paper fasteners and string.

Cut a piece of card big enough to wrap round your gift and cut 2 card circles (about the size of a 2p piece). Tie a tiny loop in one end of the string. Now push a paper fastener through one card circle, loop the string round and then push it into one edge of the card wrapping. Use another paper fastener to attach the remaining circle to the card wrap about 10cm away from the other edge.

Tie your parcel shut by looping the string under the card discs, going from one side to the other in a figure of eight. Cover the paper fasteners with sticky star shapes.

WHAT A SWEETIE!

Add a little extra to your pressies by using sweets instead of bows. Any sweets wrapped with twisted ends will do — we used fruit drops. Use ribbon round the ends of the wrappings to tie the sweets into bunches (about three to a bunch is fine). Now just tie the bunches to the ribbon tied round the parcel. Curl the ends of the ribbon by wrapping them round a pencil.

STAMP IT!

Try designing your own paper by stamping a pattern on plain brown wrap. You can buy stamps ready-made or make your own. An easy way to make a stamp is to use a Christmas cookie cutter to cut a shape from a soft, rubber eraser. Glue the shape onto some thick card and your stamp is ready. You can also cut shapes in a potato half and use that. Use a brush to put a light layer of paint on the surface of the stamp — too much paint and you'll get blobs.

POP!

Bubble wrap gives your pressies a funky, spacy look. Wrap them first in plain tissue or crepe paper. Now just wrap them again in bubble wrap (buy it at the Post Office or stationery stores). Add a bow or decoration to finish.

When things get boring after Christmas dinner, you can have loadsa fun (and annoy the Olds) popping the bubbles.

More on next page

TWINKLY TINSEL

This is especially great for small pressies. Wrap your pressie in plain paper. Now just snip a small piece of tinsel (5-6cm will do), wrap it round your finger to make a circle and stick it to the parcel with double-sided sticky tape.

If you buy an ordinary 2m tinsel garland, it will be long enough for 35-40 presents — much cheaper than buying bows.

JINGLE BELLS

Wrap your pressies as normal and add ribbon. For a change, we tied our ribbon across the corners instead of across the middle. Now just tie little bells (from fabric stores from about 5p each) to the ribbon ends.

If you like, you could use old beads instead of bells.

SCRUNCHY

Coloured tissue is brilliant for wrapping odd shaped pressies. Just plonk the pressie in the middle of the tissue, scrunch the paper around it and tie with some ribbon.

Instead of tissue, you could also try coloured net. Get it for around 70p per metre from fabric stores. Or use the net that the Christmas oranges come in — just remember to open it carefully by snipping the top off.

107

And —

Next day —

Later —

108

I'M NOT LOOKING FORWARD TO THIS WEEK. ELAINE'S AWAY ON HOLIDAY, SO I'LL HAVE NO-ONE TO TALK TO.

I'D LIKE SOMEONE TO CLEAR OUT THESE CUPBOARDS AT LUNCHTIME. ANY OFFERS?

I'LL DO IT, SIR!

IT'LL BE BETTER THAN HANGING AROUND ON MY OWN.

UGH! THESE BOOKS ARE *FILTHY!* OH, WHAT'S THAT IN THE CORNER?

IT'S THE CRIB SHEET FROM THE GEOGRAPHY TEST. AND THERE'S SOME WRITING ON THE BACK. 'LEONARDO RULES'. OH, AND AN ADDRESS AND A DATE — IT LOOKS LIKE SOMEONE'S BIRTHDAY.

MAYBE WE *CAN* FIND OUT WHO CHEATED! IT'LL BE SOMEONE WITH THIS BIRTHDAY WHO LIVES IN BEDFORD STREET AND LIKES LEONARDO DICAPRIO. DEAD EASY!

109

112

THE END

Christmas Cookies

Mmm! These Christmas Cookies are easy to make, delish and have a cool stained glass window effect.

WHAT YOU NEED

(makes around 12 biscuits)

75g Butter or margarine (softened)
75g Caster sugar
50g Custard powder
150g Self-raising flour
1 Large egg, beaten
6-8 Hard, fruity sweets

Large and small cookie cutters.

WHAT TO DO

1. Beat the butter and sugar together till the mix is light coloured and fluffy.
2. Beat in the egg.
3. Sift the flour and custard powder into the mix and stir until you have a soft dough. Wrap the dough in cling-film and chill in the fridge for at least 20 minutes.
4. Roll out the dough on a lightly floured surface. Now cut out your cookie shapes — we used a Christmas tree shape.
5. Place the cookies on a lightly greased baking tray. Now use the small cutter (we used a heart) to cut shapes from the centre of your cookies. Don't cut too close to the edge. You can bake the bits you cut out, too.

6. Now for the fun bit. Using a rolling pin or hammer, break the sweets into small pieces (watch your fingers!). Place a few of the broken pieces into the cut-out shapes.
7. Bake your cookies at 180°C/350°F/Gas Mark 4 for 15-20 minutes until they are lightly golden. The sweets in the middle will melt and make the stained glass windows. Leave on the trays until they are cool.
8. Now you can decorate your cookies. We used ready-coloured icing in tubes to make tree baubles. You could also use silver balls or cover the cookies with water icing and sugar sprinkles.

TIP: If you make holes in your cookies before you bake them, they can be threaded with ribbon and hung on the tree.

Remember to ask an adult before using any kitchen equipment.

SAFARI

The Four Marys

THE FOUR MARYS, Cotter, Field, Radleigh and Simpson, were doing some Christmas shopping in Elmbury —

MERRY CHRISTMAS

SALE

½ PRICE

OH, LOOK! IT'S ANT AND STEVE FROM ST BARTOPH'S.

GREAT! ANT'S GORGEOUS!

St Bartoph's was a neighbouring boys' boarding school.

HI! I'M CERTAINLY PLEASED TO SEE *YOU*!

ME? *REALLY*?

YEAH. I'VE NO IDEA WHAT TO GET MY SISTER FOR CHRISTMAS, SO IF YOU'VE ANY IDEAS, I'D BE REALLY GRATEFUL.

AND *I* DON'T KNOW WHAT TO GET FOR MY MUM.

OH, COME ON, THEN — WE'LL HELP YOU LOOK!

Later, in the café —

THAT WAS BRILLANT — THANKS VERY MUCH.

NO PROBLEM! BUT WE'D BETTER GET GOING.

115

When the girls got back to St Elmo's —

OH, THERE'S LOUISE. LET'S SAY HI!

SHE'LL PROBABLY WAIT FOR US IN THE BIKE SHED. IT'S TOO COLD TO HANG ABOUT OUT HERE.

BIKE SHED

AW, SHE'S GONE! SHE WAS QUICK!

WE'D BETTER BE QUICK, TOO — OR WE'LL HAVE CREEFY AFTER US!

Later —

A BABY'S BEEN STOLEN FROM A PRAM IN ELMBURY! IT'S ON ALL THE LOCAL NEWS PROGRAMMES!

WHAT? THAT'S AWFUL!

LITTLE EMMA WAS WEARING A PINK SNOWSUIT. THE POLICE ARE CONDUCTING A SEARCH . . .

SHE'LL NEED HER SNOWSUIT IN THIS WEATHER — POOR THING!

THE STRANGE THING IS, THE BABY WAS TAKEN FROM OUTSIDE THE CAFE — ABOUT THE SAME TIME WE WERE THERE . . .

SO MAYBE WE CAN HELP FIND HER!

HOW ABOUT GOING BACK TO THE CAFE TOMORROW?

GOOD IDEA, FIELDY!

Next day —

CAFE

WE WERE SITTING OVER THERE, QUITE NEAR THE WINDOW, BUT I DON'T REMEMBER SEEING ANYTHING UNUSUAL.

ME, NEITHER!

MIND YOU, WE *WERE* BUSY TALKING TO ANT AND STEVE. MAYBE I SHOULD PHONE THEM TO SEE IF *THEY* NOTICED ANYTHING?

YEAH — WHY NOT?

So —

TELEPHONE

LTD

ANY LUCK?

NO. *THEY'VE* HEARD THE NEWS, TOO, BUT THEY DON'T REMEMBER SEEING ANYTHING.

WE COULD ASK IN THE CAFE — THE STAFF, OR SOME OF THE REGULARS MAY HAVE SEEN SOMETHING.

But —

Menu.

THE POLICE HAVE ALREADY SPOKEN TO US. I GAVE THEM THE NAMES OF THE CUSTOMERS WE COULD REMEMBER, BUT I FORGOT ABOUT YOU.

WE CAN'T HELP ANYWAY. WE'VE BEEN TRYING TO THINK BUT WE'VE NOT COME UP WITH ANYTHING.

WELL, AT LEAST WE TRIED.

YEAH AND THE POLICE ARE DOING EVERYTHING POSSIBLE.

IT'LL BE IN THE LOCAL PAPER, TOO, WHICH MIGHT JOG A FEW MEMORIES. WE SHOULD HAVE BOUGHT ONE.

IT LOOKS LIKE LOUISE HAS ONE — I'M SURE SHE'LL LET US SEE IT.

CAN I HAND IT IN TO YOU LATER? I'M IN A HURRY.

YEAH, SURE, LOUISE.

WHAT WERE ALL THOSE LITTLE TINS RATTLING IN HER BAG?

WHO KNOWS? MAYBE SHE'S HAVING A PARTY.

SHE SEEMED A BIT FLUSTERED. I HOPE SHE'S OKAY.

Later —

THERE'S LOUISE AGAIN. WHERE'S SHE GOING WITH THAT RUCKSACK?

SICK BAY →

IT LOOKS LIKE SHE'S GOING TO THE SICK BAY.

BUT WHY?

SSSH, SHE'S COMING OUT AGAIN.

SICK BAY

LOOK, I KNOW THIS SOUNDS CRAZY . . .

. . . BUT DO YOU THINK IT COULD BE *LOUISE* WHO TOOK THAT BABY? MAYBE SHE'S HIDING IT HERE IN THE SCHOOL! THAT COULD BE WHY SHE WANTS BLANKETS AND THOSE TINS THAT WERE IN HER BAG MIGHT BE BABY FOOD!

IT ALL FITS. THAT TIME WE EXPECTED HER TO BE WAITING FOR US IN THE BIKE SHED WAS JUST AFTER THE BABY WENT MISSING!

119

PENNY'S PLACE

PENNY JORDAN was helping her parents decorate Penny's Place, their café in Chesterford.

TODAY'S SPECIAL

I CAN'T BELIEVE IT'S ONLY *TWO* WEEKS TILL CHRISTMAS, DAD!

HOW ABOUT HAVING A CHRISTMAS PARTY HERE FOR THE LOCAL KIDS?

A KIDS' PARTY? YOU MUST BE JOKING, LOVE!

WE'LL HAVE ENOUGH TO DO WITH ALL OUR REGULAR CUSTOMERS, PENNY.

Then Sita, Arlene and Gemma arrived —

HI, PENNY! COMING CHRISTMAS SHOPPING WITH US?

SURE!

THE KIDS ROUND HERE WOULD HAVE LOVED A PARTY. BUT MUM AND DAD ARE RIGHT — IT'S *ALWAYS* BUSY AT CHRISTMAS!

JUST A MOMENT, PENNY. DON'T FORGET WE'VE GOT TO BUY YOU NEW SCHOOL SHOES THIS AFTERNOON.

121

AW, MUM! CAN'T WE GO *ANOTHER* DAY?

NO. WE'LL HAVE TO GO TODAY WHEN THE CAFE'S CLOSED. BUT I SUPPOSE WE COULD MEET YOU LATER.

HOW ABOUT FOUR O'CLOCK BY THE SHOE DEPARTMENT AT ILLINGHAMS?

COOL! THANKS, MUM!

So, in town —

EVERYTHING'S SO EXPENSIVE. I WANTED TO BUY A GLASS ORNAMENT FOR MUM, BUT I CAN'T AFFORD ANYTHING HERE.

ME NEITHER. THIS PERFUME'S LOVELY — BUT IT COSTS TOO MUCH!

LET'S TRY ILLINGHAMS. THERE'S A SALE ON THERE.

YEAH — WE'RE WASTING OUR TIME IN HERE.

A few minutes later, at Illinghams —

OH — THERE'S DONNA.

HI, DONNA!

ARE YOU CHRISTMAS SHOPPING, TOO?

YEAH! I'M TAKING KYLIE TO SEE SANTA!

122

123

THAT'S AWFUL! THREE POUNDS FOR HALF A MINUTE WITH SANTA AND A CHEAP LITTLE PLASTIC TOY.

YEAH! IT'S NOT FAIR. THE OTHER KIDS ARE DISAPPOINTED, TOO. I THINK YOU SHOULD COMPLAIN, DONNA.

WHAT'S THE USE? IT'D ONLY SPOIL THINGS EVEN MORE FOR KYLIE IF I MADE A FUSS. I'LL BUY HER SOMETHING ELSE TO MAKE UP FOR IT.

OOPS! IT'S NEARLY FOUR O'CLOCK. I'D BETTER GO AND MEET MUM AND DAD.

POOR LITTLE KYLIE! THAT'S SO UNFAIR, DISAPPOINTING HER LIKE THAT.

Later —

SANTA'S GROTTO'S A REAL RIP-OFF. THEY'RE CHARGING THREE POUNDS AND THE KIDS ARE HARDLY IN THERE BEFORE THEY'RE PUSHED OUT AGAIN WITH A CHEAP LITTLE TOY. I DON'T THINK IT'S FAIR.

YOU'RE RIGHT, PENNY. THAT IS A RIP-OFF! I'M GOING TO SPEAK TO THE MANAGER ABOUT IT!

So —

I HAVE TO SAY THAT YOU'RE THE FIRST PERSON TO COMPLAIN, SIR. EVERYONE ELSE APPEARS TO BE SATISFIED.

HAVE YOU SEEN THE KIDS? THEY CERTAINLY AREN'T SATISFIED! IT'S A RIP-OFF. YOU AREN'T GIVING VALUE FOR MONEY AND YOU KNOW IT!

124

farTASTIC!

We promised you more, didn't we? And we always keep our promises, so here they are.
● Remember that SAE or INTERNATIONAL REPLY COUPON if you're writing to an address abroad.

Will Smith,
c/o CAA,
9830 Wilshire Blvd.,
Beverly Hills,
CA 90212
U.S.A.

X-Files,
c/o Fox TV,
10201 West Pico Blvd,
Los Angeles,
CA 90035,
U.S.A.

Kavana,
Fan Club Services,
P.O. Box 20,
Manchester
M60 3ED.

Mariah Carey,
P.O. Box 679,
Brandford,
Connecticut 06405,
U.S.A.

Billy Crawford,
3 Alveston Place,
Leamington Spa
CV32 4SN.

The Gary Barlow Official Fan Club,
P.O. Box 153,
Stanmore,
Middlesex
HA7 2HF.

Janet Jackson,
Friends of Janet,
P.O. Box 11306,
London
WC1E 7AJ.

911,
P.O. Box 911,
Glasgow
G1 3PQ.

The Official Cleopatra Fan Club,
P.O. Box 333,
Glasgow
G5 9YH.